The Desert War

James Holland

with illustrations by
Keith Burns

T0333013

Ladybird Books Ltd, London

At 6 p.m. on 10 June 1940, Benito Mussolini, the Fascist dictator of Italy, appeared on the balcony of the Palazzo Venezia in Rome and declared war against Britain and France. Crowds had gathered below but, although a few rabble-rousers had been planted there, for the most part the people remained silent. 'People of Italy,' he shouted, 'rush to arms and show your tenacity, your courage, your valour!' Although plenty of young Italians were filled with excitement, they were the minority. 'The news of war,' noted Mussolini's son-in-law and Foreign Minister, Count Galeazzo Ciano, in his diary, 'does not arouse much enthusiasm. I am sad, very sad. The adventure begins. May God help Italy.'

This was a huge gamble by Mussolini. Italy lacked natural resources and geographically was locked into the Mediterranean. Its industry was underdeveloped, far more so than that of Britain, France or Germany, and nor was it anything like as wealthy. On the other hand, its population was growing, although 47 per cent of the Italian workforce was employed in agriculture, which was also backward.

In May 1939, Mussolini had signed the Pact of Steel with Germany, which began the Axis alliance, even though Italy was dependent on Britain and France for 80 per cent of her seaborne imports. Clearly, Nazi Germany had her own expansionist aims, but so too had Mussolini: he hoped to create a new Roman Empire across the Mediterranean and into Africa; Abyssinia in East Africa, for example, had already been conquered. Overseas expansion offered a solution to his country's lack of resources, while an alliance with Hitler and the Nazis ensured Germany would not become Italy's enemy again as she had been during the last war.

Mussolini on the balcony of the Palazzo Venezia.

Series 117

This is a Ladybird Expert book, one of a series of titles for an adult readership. Written by some of the leading lights and outstanding communicators in their fields and published by one of the most trusted and well-loved names in books, the Ladybird Expert series provides clear, accessible and authoritative introductions, informed by expert opinion, to key subjects drawn from science, history and culture.

Every effort has been made to ensure images are correctly attributed; however, if any omission or error has been made please notify the Publisher for correction in future editions.

MICHAEL JOSEPH

UK | USA | Canada | Ireland | Australia
India | New Zealand | South Africa

Michael Joseph is part of the Penguin Random House group of companies whose addresses can be found at global.penguinrandomhouse.com

First published 2018

001

Text copyright © James Holland, 2018

All images copyright © Ladybird Books Ltd, 2018

The moral right of the author has been asserted

Printed in Italy by L.E.G.O. S.p.A.

A CIP catalogue record for this book is available from the British Library

ISBN: 978–0–718–18650–0

www.greenpenguin.co.uk

Mussolini had chosen the timing of his declaration of war carefully. His armed forces were weak, but he feared that Germany could dominate all Europe and take on all France's – and Britain's – overseas possessions in Africa. Italy's influence would rapidly dwindle to the point where she became little more than a vassal state.

Therefore he felt he had no choice but to enter the war before the fighting was over. By 10 June, France was all but finished and, as far as Mussolini was concerned, Britain looked likely to follow. In other words, there was now a good chance Italy could gain much for not a huge amount, and the number-one target was Egypt, not directly part of the British Empire but a 'protectorate' in which British armed forces were able to base themselves and control the vital Suez Canal that linked the Mediterranean to the Indian Ocean.

The trouble was, for all Fascist Italy's military parades and chest-puffing, any impression of military strength was a charade. The lack of wealth and resources was a big problem, but so too was excessive bureaucracy and the low calibre of senior leadership. The Regio Esercito – Royal Army, as Italy still had a king, despite Fascism – was short of tanks, artillery, vehicles, rifles and just about everything needed for modern warfare. The Regia Aeronautica – Royal Air Force – was also filled with outmoded aircraft and inept commanders, while the Regia Marina – Royal Navy – the most modern arm, lacked any aircraft carriers or any kind of radar and, most of all, experience.

There was also a pointed lack of enthusiasm for war from Italy's military commanders. Only Mussolini himself, it seemed, had much appetite for a scrap with the British.

From 11 June onwards, Italian bombers began half-heartedly attacking the tiny but strategically vital British island of Malta in the very heart of the Mediterranean. The island was woefully under-defended with just a handful of Gloster Gladiator biplanes and almost no anti-aircraft guns, but the Italians never pressed home their advantage. The British swiftly reinforced the island. Within ten days, Hurricanes had begun arriving and by the end of the year it was bristling with anti-aircraft guns as well as bombers and submarines. Malta had become a major thorn in the Italians' side and an offensive base from which the British could attack Axis convoys heading to Libya.

Then, in July 1940, the Regia Marina ventured out of port and clashed with the British Mediterranean Fleet, receiving a bloody nose for its trouble. Finally, on Friday, 13 September, after continual pressing from Mussolini, Marshal Rodolfo Graziani reluctantly ordered the Italian Tenth Army to cross the Libyan border into Egypt. It advanced 40 miles to Sidi Barrani then halted.

The armed forces were mired in labyrinthine bureaucracy. On the outbreak of war, the Ministry Secretariat, the mechanism of government, had agreed to extend its working day to 4 p.m., but by July a return to the old time of 2 p.m. had been proposed and agreed. Marshal Pietro Badoglio, the Chief of Staff and most senior Italian soldier, was sixty-eight years old and rooted in the past. When handed a perceptive analysis of German tactics, he said, 'We'll study it when the war is over.' Command was top-heavy, training rigid and initiative stifled from top to bottom. 'The tank is a powerful tool,' said General Ettore Bastico, another senior commander, 'but let us not idolize it. Let us reserve our reverence for the infantryman and the mule.'

An Italian SM-79 Sparviero being shot down by RAF Spitfires over Malta.

Britain's determination to keep fighting and her victory in the Battle of Britain was throwing Mussolini's war plans awry. The Italian Navy was proving feckless, so too was Graziani's Tenth Army in Egypt, and Italy was already running short of food. A mass demobilization of some 750,000 men was ordered because many of the peasant soldiers were urgently needed back on the land.

Despite this, on 12 October German troops moved into Romania, fuelling Il Duce's paranoia about German domination in what he considered his own patch. Mussolini was incensed. He had a bullying, dominant ally with a string of victories under its belt, while Britain, supposed to be dead and buried, was getting stronger by the day. So far nothing had gone to plan, but a quick and easy victory over the Greeks could change all that and reassert Italian dominance in the Mediterranean.

On 28 October, Italian forces invaded Greece from Albania and from across the sea. Poorly equipped and without their supply chain properly thought through, the Italians struggled in the mountainous interior and against a determined Greek Army that was ten times the size Mussolini had thought. Within a week, the campaign was unravelling and the Italians falling back.

On 11 November, they suffered a further humiliation when Royal Navy Fleet Air Arm Swordfish attacked the Italian Fleet at harbour in Taranto. Malta-based RAF reconnaissance aircraft had accurately spotted six battleships there. In the night-time attack two were sunk and a third severely damaged, along with a cruiser and destroyer. Half the Italian battle fleet had been put out of action in one brilliantly executed attack.

Operation JUDGEMENT: the Royal Navy's night attack on Taranto.

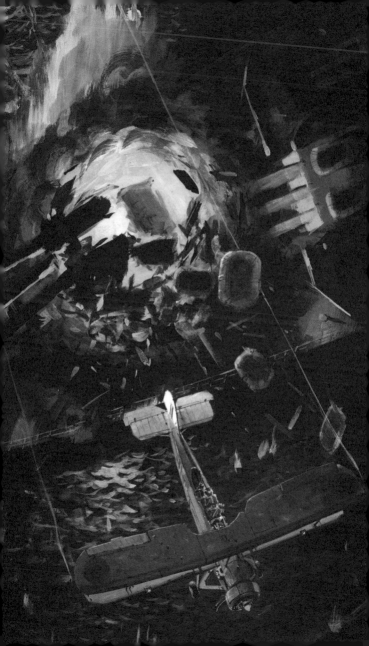

While the British Mediterranean Fleet had been giving the Italian Navy a bloody nose, it was clear there was now a chance to blunt Mussolini's ambitions in Africa too and make the Italians even more of a liability to Germany. Winston Churchill, the British Prime Minister, had been urging General Sir Archibald Wavell, the Commander-in-Chief Middle East, to go on the offensive in Egypt. Since October, the British Western Desert Force, only 36,000 strong and commanded by General Dick O'Connor, had been harrying Italian positions. Among those carrying out raids to capture prisoners and harass the Italians was Albert Martin, a young rifleman in 2nd Rifle Brigade. Beetling about the desert in their six-man trucks, he and his mates were able to lie up their truck then easily creep up on the Italians by night. 'We had total freedom of movement,' he noted, 'the Italians preferring to stay in their defensive enclaves.'

On the night of 8 December, the British attacked in force in what was called Operation COMPASS. They achieved complete surprise, and just three days later the Italian positions had been overrun, Sidi Barrani retaken and 38,300 prisoners captured along with 237 guns and 73 tanks. Rarely had a battle gone so completely to plan.

By 20 December, the Italians had been swept out of Egypt and were on the run, with Albert Martin and the rest of the Western Desert Force in hot pursuit, led by the 6th Australian Division. Mussolini hadn't taken on just Britain but her Dominion countries too.

A six-man section in a 15-cwt truck crossing the desert.

Now fearing complete Italian collapse, which would have left his southern flank vulnerable, Hitler ordered reinforcements to Africa to shore up his allies. To ensure they crossed the Mediterranean safely, however, an entire Luftwaffe air corps, Fliegerkorps X, was posted to Sicily in order to attack and neutralize the British Mediterranean Fleet. After severely damaging the aircraft carrier *Illustrious*, the Luftwaffe then pounded Malta, where the ship had limped for repairs. The damage to the island was unlike anything experienced at the hands of the Regia Aeronautica, but *Illustrious* did successfully get away from the island and make for Alexandria.

Malta had been blunted as an offensive base, however, and two German divisions under Major-General Erwin Rommel reached Tripoli in February 1941. By this time, the Western Desert Force had smashed the Italians. The Libyan towns of Bardia, Tobruk and Benghazi had all fallen, with the British using the same tactics the Germans had used in France the previous May: enemy airfields were hammered in advance, then mobile troops surged forward and encircled their enemy. On 12 February, the day Rommel reached Tripoli, the British took a further 20,000 Italian POWs, 200 guns and 120 tanks. The Italian Tenth Army had been destroyed and some 130,000 troops captured. 'Never has so much been surrendered to so few,' joked Anthony Eden, the British Foreign Secretary.

Meanwhile, Hitler had also decided to come to the Italians' rescue in Greece. His biggest concern was the possible loss of the vital Romanian oilfields at Ploeşti. With the Balkans and Aegean under Axis control, these would be secure.

Stukas dive-bombing HMS *Illustrious* in Grand Harbour, Malta.

The British, meanwhile, were also being drawn into Greece. They had promised to guarantee Greek independence back in April 1939, and had already sent naval and air support and had pledged troops too should Germany ever intervene. Troops for Greece would mean reducing those in Libya as British forces were also now attacking the Italians in East Africa. On the other hand, with the Italians cut off in East Africa, in retreat in Greece and already badly mauled in North Africa, the British felt they were ripe for the plucking. Another attack was launched to drive them even further west in North Africa and once again, Mussolini's men were soon in retreat.

The Italian Navy was also further hammered when the fleet ventured from port to try to stop British shipping to Greece. After a brief chase, the British Mediterranean Fleet closed in on the night of 28/29 March to around 4,000 yards of the Italians – effectively point-blank range. The British commander, Admiral Andrew Browne Cunningham, known to all as 'ABC', gave the order for his fleet to engage the enemy for the first time since Nelson's day. 'Never,' he wrote, 'have I experienced a more thrilling moment.' It was a massacre. All three Italian cruisers were sunk. The Battle of Cape Matapan ensured the Italian Fleet would never threaten British naval supremacy in the Mediterranean again.

While Matapan was raging, Yugoslavia was in turmoil. First the country joined the Axis, then there was a coup and the decision reversed. Hitler's revenge was swift. On 6 April 1941, the Germans invaded both Yugoslavia and Greece simultaneously.

The Mediterranean Fleet opening fire at the start of the night action off Cape Matapan.

General Rommel had been told to stabilize the front in Libya and under no circumstances go on the attack, but he ignored this order. With the Western Desert Force now weakened by the Greek venture, he swiftly advanced back across Cyrenaica in Libya, retaking Benghazi and Bardia and besieging Tobruk. He also managed to capture the British commander, General O'Connor.

On 17 April, Yugoslavia surrendered, while the Germans swiftly advanced in Greece, where the Italians had so badly failed. Britain had sent four divisions, which had been hastily brought into battle, although without enough coordination with their Greek allies. It was too little too late, while in the air the Luftwaffe reigned supreme. The future novelist Roald Dahl was one of the few RAF fighter pilots trying to stem the flow, but he and his fellows were horribly outnumbered. Soon both the British and Greeks were in full retreat. Fortunately, the majority of British troops were successfully evacuated, but next on Germany's list was the large island of Crete. There were now some 32,000 British, Australian and New Zealand troops there, as well as 10,000 Greek troops, which should have been enough to hold the island from the Germans.

Operation MERCURY was launched by the Germans with wave after wave of *Fallschirmjäger* – paratroopers – dropping at dawn on 20 May. They suffered catastrophic losses and the invasion should have stalled there and then. However, due to a tragic and terrible oversight, German defeat was all too swiftly turned into a stunning victory.

German paratroopers with wrecked JU-52s during Operation MERCURY.

Crete should never have fallen. General Bernard Freyberg, the New Zealander commander, was convinced a seaborne attack was also likely and so failed to reinforce the key airfield of Maleme in the west of the island. The brigade commander there also prematurely pulled his men back from the airfield and, as a result, Maleme was swiftly captured by the Germans then hurriedly reinforced with *Gebirgsjäger* – mountain troops – flown in directly. The die had been cast and the Germans were able to rapidly build up strength and push the defenders back. By 27 May, another British evacuation had begun and, although the vast majority were successfully lifted, the island was surrendered on 1 July. It was a humiliating defeat, but a costly victory for the Germans. The elite *Fallschirmjäger* units had lost more than 6,000 men, as well as 143 precious transport planes and a further 120 severely damaged. With the invasion of the Soviet Union a few weeks away, these were disastrous losses – and for little strategic gain.

The British Royal Navy suffered badly too: three cruisers and six destroyers were lost during the evacuation. The vital importance of air power and close air support had become ever more obvious during the Greek and Cretan ventures.

On the plus side, the Italians were, by the end of May, all but defeated in Abyssinia, and the island fortress of Malta was once more proving a vital offensive base. On 24 May, the British submarine HMS *Upholder* broke into an Italian destroyer screen and sank the massive 18,000-ton troopship *Conte Rosso* – for which *Upholder*'s captain, Lieutenant-Commander David Wanklyn, was awarded a VC. The Malta submarines were starting to prove a major scourge for Axis shipping. Capturing Malta would have proved a more profitable target for Hitler than Crete.

HMS *Upholder* arrives back in Malta after another successful patrol

In much the same way that Germany swept into the Balkans and Greece to prevent the British from doing the same, so the British now became determined to stop German interference in the Middle East. The first objective was Syria, currently held by Vichy – pro-Axis – France. RAF possession of Syrian airfields would counteract any Luftwaffe presence on Crete. Churchill instructed General Wavell to mount a joint attack with General Charles de Gaulle's small Free French forces in early June.

At the same time, Wavell was anxious to push back Rommel and relieve the port of Tobruk, where the mostly Australian troops were still holding out. Just to make life even harder for Wavell, Rashid Ali al-Gaylani had mounted a pro-Axis coup in Iraq. Britain controlled a vast swathe of territory from Palestine to India and having an openly hostile political leader in Iraq at this time was intolerable. Troops were sent from India and air forces from RAF Middle East, and the rising was quickly quelled, but after the defeats of Greece and Crete Wavell's Middle East Command was horribly overstretched. Operation EXPORTER, the battle for Syria, was launched on 8 June, while Operation BATTLEAXE, in the Western Desert in Egypt, began a week later, on the 15th. As was now so often proving the way for the British in the Mediterranean and Middle East, fortunes ebbed and flowed.

After three days of intense and blisteringly hot battle with little progress being made, Wavell was forced to call off BATTLEAXE with Tobruk still out of reach. There was better news in Syria, however. On 21 June, Damascus fell, and three weeks later, on 11 July, the Vichy French surrendered. The Eastern Mediterranean was now secure.

Moscow

Soviet
Union

800 km

0   500 miles

Istanbul

Greece   Turkey

Athens

Crete

Syria   Tehran

Damascus   Baghdad   Iran

Tobruk   Palestine   Iraq

El Alamein   Trans
          Jordan
Cairo

Libya

Egypt   Riyadh

Saudi Arabia   Oman

Anglo-Egyptian
Sudan

Chad   Eritrea   Yemen   Aden
Khartoum   Protectorate

Abyssinia

Addis Ababa

Ubangi-Shari

Germany invaded the Soviet Union on 21 June 1941. At the same time, German spies were agitating dissent against the British in Iran, which threatened Britain's aid route to Russia through the Persian Gulf. When the British and Soviets jointly demanded the expulsion of all German nationals, the Tehran government refused. On 25 August a joint Anglo-Russian force invaded Iran, occupied Tehran, and the Persian Gulf was secured. East Africa was now almost entirely in British hands; the Middle East all the way to India was secure; and, despite the defeats in Crete and Greece, the British command in the Mediterranean and Middle East theatre was now finally free to concentrate its efforts on North Africa.

General Wavell, however, had been sacked as British C-in-C. His had been a thankless task and he had been horribly overstretched, but Churchill correctly sensed that he lacked the people skills and dynamic flair that was needed. Wavell was replaced by General Claude Auchinleck, who had been C-in-C India. 'The Auk', as he was known, arrived as more reinforcements were reaching Egypt and strength growing. In September, his forces were entirely reorganized. Tenth Army was formed in Iraq, Ninth Army in Palestine and Eighth Army in Egypt under command of Lieutenant-General Alan Cunningham, brother of the admiral and fresh from victory in Abyssinia.

Meanwhile, the Germans continued to boss their Axis ally in Libya. Rommel now took command of the Panzer Group Afrika, which included both German and Italian forces. He was supposed to be answerable to the Italians, but paid them scant regard.

Rommel in his command car passing troops of the Afrikakorps

Rommel's men were still trying to bludgeon Tobruk into submission, but the besieged outpost held firm. Both sides were now preparing for a major offensive. For Eighth Army, the first objective was the relief of Tobruk. For the Axis forces, it was breaking the stubborn siege and pushing the British out of Egypt. Of vital importance was the smooth flow of supplies to both sides. While British shipping had the longer route, it was arriving largely untroubled. The same could not be said for Axis shipping across the Mediterranean, which was now being pummelled by Malta-based aircraft, ships and submarines in particular.

In November 1941, for example, submarines, ships and aircraft operating from the island destroyed 77 per cent of all Axis convoys heading across the Mediterranean. Malta's submarines, such as HMS *Upholder*, were sinking not only huge amounts of enemy shipping but also some of the largest supply vessels in the Axis arsenal – ships that could not be replaced. Force K, a group of fast cruisers and destroyers, managed to annihilate one Axis convoy of ten merchant vessels and six Italian destroyers; all but three destroyers were sunk. Malta's aircraft also bombed and torpedoed enemy shipping. Hitler was so incensed that he ordered U-boats to be diverted from the critical Atlantic and into the Mediterranean instead.

It was Eighth Army who struck first in North Africa, on 18 November in what was called Operation CRUSADER. By this time, the British had three times as many tanks and double the number of aircraft as their opponents. What followed was three hard weeks of bloody and confusing battle.

RAF Beaufighters attacking an Axis merchant vessel.

'In all directions came the noise of battle,' noted Albert Martin of 2nd Rifle Brigade, 'twenty-five pounders crashing away just yards off, a cluster of tanks in the distance firing at something, but whether they were friend or foe was difficult to make out; neither could I work out what the target was.' Martin and his comrades were in lightly armoured tracked carriers, but this was a battle of tanks and guns. At one point some panzers rumbled past amid clouds of swirling dust but didn't shoot at the riflemen. Only at dusk did the fighting die down.

Rommel had been caught off-guard by the attack and, misreading the situation, had sent his panzer divisions towards Bardia. In fact, most of the British tanks were further to the south and so were then able to drive up towards Tobruk. Rommel realized his mistake, ordered an about-turn and the two sides clashed at Sidi Rezegh, 10 miles to the south-east of the town, in what was the biggest tank battle of the North African campaign so far. 'Dust, smoke, burning oil, exploding shell and debris filled the air,' wrote Australian journalist Alan Moorehead. 'From a distance, it was merely noise and confusion.'

Over the next couple of days it was high-velocity German anti-tank guns rather than panzers that halted the British advance. Rommel then attempted to drive eastwards again and Cunningham stopped his offensive. Auchinleck overruled then sacked him, replacing him with his own Chief of Staff in Cairo, Major-General Neil Ritchie. The battle would continue after all.

The panzers were now overstretched and being pummelled by the RAF's Desert Air Force, while the British had pushed forward and finally relieved Tobruk. Rommel tried to counter-attack but could make no headway against strong defence: it was now the turn of British artillery and anti-tank guns to halt the Axis armour. When the Italian Motorized Corps failed to join the attack on Tobruk on 5 December, Rommel accepted it was time to pull back. After one final assault on 7 December, he broke off and his battered forces sped back across the bulge of Cyrenaica. So the see-saw North Africa campaign continued.

Meanwhile, across the Mediterranean, Malta was soon to feel the wrath of the Luftwaffe once more. No one was more obsessed with the Mediterranean than Hitler, who constantly feared for his southern flank. With faith in his Italian ally completely gone, he now sent Field Marshal Albert Kesselring to command all Axis forces in the south.

Kesselring was known as 'Smiling Albert' because of his cheery manner, but this hid a grim ruthlessness and devout allegiance to the Führer. He correctly understood that the war in North Africa would be won or lost by whichever side won the battle of supplies, so with this in mind he determined to crush Malta as an offensive base.

Fliegerkorps II arrived on Sicily in December and in the New Year began pummelling the island. Over the next four months, its cities and harbours were smashed, airfields wrecked and air forces all but destroyed. Malta was an offensive base no more. It had become the most bombed place on earth.

The Luftwaffe bombing Malta.

Both Kesselring and the Italian High Command had hoped to follow the Malta blitz with an invasion, but Rommel was keen to seize the initiative in North Africa and drive the British out of Libya then Egypt, and there were not enough men or aircraft to do both at once. In the Soviet Union, the Germans were also planning a drive towards the Caucasus in the south-east. Rommel's flair and ambition appealed to Hitler, who now dreamed of linking up both forces through the Middle East. This was pure fantasy, but it meant an invasion of Malta would have to wait.

Rommel attacked on 26 May. Eighth Army was strung out over 40 miles of desert, from the Mediterranean to the Free French outpost of Bir Hacheim in what was called the Gazala Line. Infantry were placed in 'boxes' surrounded by wire entanglements and minefields and often separated from one another by a number of miles. Behind were the mobile units, such as those of Albert Martin and his fellows, and the British tank units. General Ritchie's dispositions made little sense, as behind was Tobruk, a garrison that had held out for nine months the previous year and already had defences in place. Rommel could have bypassed the town, but not for long, because the British in Tobruk would easily have been able to strangle his supply lines. This meant he would have had to turn and deal with Tobruk before charging off into Egypt and the Middle East.

Instead, he simply sent his mobile forces, including the Deutsches Afrikakorps, around the southern flank of the Gazala Line and came in around the back of the British positions.

The Afrikakorps on the march.

Even then, Eighth Army had the chance to encircle Rommel's armour and crush him in turn, but chronic dithering at the top and a lack of firm and resolute generalship from Ritchie and his corps commanders ensured a golden opportunity to smash the German forces for good went begging. Instead, the Axis were able to dramatically regain the initiative and pick off Eighth Army units in detail, one by one. The 'Cauldron', a wide, shallow depression in the desert, became a scene of carnage as the British armour was largely destroyed by screens of anti-tank guns. Soon Eighth Army was in full retreat and then, on 21 June, Tobruk was surrounded and forced to surrender. It was a devastating and humiliating blow. British generalship at Gazala had been abject.

Eighth Army now streamed back into Egypt and to the Alamein position. This lay some 60 miles west of Alexandria and was almost the only place in the Western Desert that could not be outflanked because of the deep Qattara Depression some 40 miles to the south. What saved Eighth Army from annihilation was the Desert Air Force, who flew round-the-clock missions harrying the enemy at every turn and leap-frogging backwards from one desert landing ground to another. Since the fall of France in 1940, the RAF had been learning important lessons about how to provide close air support effectively to land forces. Men like Air Chief Marshal Arthur Tedder and the commander of the Desert Air Force, Air Vice-Marshal Arthur 'Mary' Coningham, were dynamic, charismatic and forward-thinking, and well served by tough, battle-hardened young squadron commanders. The contrast with Eighth Army's generals could not have been starker.

112 'Shark' Squadron P-40 Kittyhawks
shooting up an Axis column.

After the loss of Tobruk, Ritchie was fired and the Auk took over direct command of Eighth Army. Throughout July, his troops managed to hold off the newly promoted Field Marshal Rommel's Panzer Army Afrika. By August, both sides were exhausted. Churchill visited Egypt in early August and Auchinleck was now sacked too. General William 'Strafer' Gott took over Eighth Army but was then killed in a deliberate air attack as he flew to Cairo. The vastly experienced General Sir Harold Alexander took over as C-in-C Middle East, while Lieutenant-General Bernard Montgomery was given command of Eighth Army. Both announced an end to any more retreats. They would build up forces, retrain their men and, when ready, attack.

On Malta, meanwhile, the RAF had wrested back the air battle thanks to the arrival of good numbers of Spitfires, but the people were starving. A convoy in March had reached the island only to be sunk in harbour, while the next, in June, had been forced to turn back. In August, the most heavily protected convoy of the war set off from Gibraltar along the length of the Mediterranean: thirteen merchantmen and one tanker, protected by four aircraft carriers, two battleships, seven cruisers and thirty-two destroyers. Against them were 600 Axis aircraft, as well as submarines and fast torpedo boats. Operation PEDESTAL was an epic. Only four of the merchant ships made it, while the tanker, *Ohio*, was hit no fewer than ten times and even a Stuka dive-bomber crashed on her decks. She finally inched into Grand Harbour on 15 August, low in the water and towed by three destroyers. Malta had been saved.

The *Ohio* limping into Malta's
Grand Harbour as Spitfires fly overhead

It has often been claimed that British equipment was inferior to that of the Germans. That was not really the case. Nor was there much wrong with training methods. Eighth Army was now filled with men who had plenty of experience of fighting in the desert. The biggest problem was one of poor morale, as both Alexander and Montgomery recognized. This was their greatest challenge, but with no-nonsense pep-talks, new Sherman tanks from the US and plenty of hard training, they were soon able to turn things around.

Living and fighting in the desert was challenging for both sides. Water was in limited supply, food was monotonous and, in the case of the Germans and Italians, barely edible. Millions of flies swarmed around the men all the time, but especially when eating. There were sand flies, scorpions and other bugs to deal with. Desert sores were rife, and all the men were a long, long way from home. Sand storms, the *khamseen*, could suddenly sweep in and bury an entire truck. Daylight hours could be blisteringly hot, but nights freezing.

Those who embraced it could thrive, as British special forces, the Long Range Desert Group and SAS, proved. Operating far behind enemy lines, the LRDG provided vital intelligence, while in the summer of 1942 the SAS proved increasingly effective, carrying out daring raids on Axis airfields and supply columns, then melting back into the desert once more. On 26 July, for example, in an attack on El Daba landing ground, the SAS destroyed thirty-seven German transport planes, all of which were vital for Rommel's efforts to rebuild strength.

The SAS, operating deep in the Western Desert, under attack from Luftwaffe ME-109s

With Malta resurgent as an offensive base, the British were able to attack Axis supply convoys from both sides of the Mediterranean and hit them hard. Many Axis ships went down that August, which was catastrophic for Rommel's new Panzer Army Afrika, especially since their lines of supply were so stretched. British supply lines were now both short and barely interrupted.

Rommel attacked on 30 August, but this time his attempted outflanking sweep was met by firm defence and by intense carpet-bombing by the RAF. 'Wave after wave of heavy bomber formations dropped their high explosive,' recalled Colonel Fritz Bayerlein, Chief of Staff of the Afrikakorps. There was no let-up, either day or night, and both Bayerlein and Rommel were lucky to survive. The German commander began pulling back his forces on 2 September. The Battle of Alam Halfa had not achieved the breakthrough for which Rommel had hoped. 'Our last chance to win in the Nile Delta,' noted Bayerlein, 'had passed.'

With the Panzer Army now on the defensive, Montgomery began readying himself for his own attack. Intensive training and an increased build-up of forces meant he was not ready until the full moon in the third week of October.

Meanwhile, back in Britain, the build-up of American forces had been continuing since America's entry into the war the previous December. The plan had been to launch a joint Anglo-US invasion of Europe, but it quickly became clear that neither the British nor the Americans were ready. A large-scale Canadian raid on Dieppe in August had been a bloody failure. A successful invasion of north-west Africa, however, was more achievable. Operation TORCH was due to launch in November, after Eighth Army attacked in the desert.

General Montgomery.

The British offensive at Alamein began on the night of 23 October after incessant air attacks and a large-scale artillery barrage. The sound and sight of this barrage remained long in the memory, but it was largely a failure. Instead of focusing much of his artillery in the north, which was where the main attack was made, Montgomery chose to spread it down the length of the line. Furthermore, instead of firing in concentrations, each gun aimed directly ahead, where the impact of the landing shells was less.

This meant few of the mines, wire or Axis defences were destroyed, and it left the massed infantry and armour to fight a grinding, attritional and costly battle. Montgomery had said the fighting would last ten days and he was quite right. It did. With different tactics, however, it might have been over in a quarter of the time. Albert Martin found himself engaged in a desperate day-long battle as an anti-tank gunner at what became known as the Snipe action, but it helped stop the German armoured counter-attack on 27 October. By the end of the day, more than sixty Axis tanks littered the desert around them.

For Italian Lieutenant Giuseppe Santaniello, it was air power, more than anything, that broke the spirits of his men and himself. 'The RAF,' he noted in his diary, 'always wins.' In truth, it was a combination of weight of arms and the grim determination of the men on the ground as well as air power that brought victory to the British. By 2 November, the Panzer Army Afrika was in full retreat.

Six days later, American troops landed in Vichy-controlled north-west Africa. The giant pincer movement to crush the Axis in Africa had begun.

The Snipe action.

Operation TORCH was, at the time, the largest amphibious operation the world had ever seen. Three separate invasion forces, one from the US and two from Britain, managed to land pretty much at the right place and on time. The Vichy French forces were quickly overrun and so the British First Army, containing the US II Corps, began its march on Tunis, while Montgomery's men snapped at the heels of the retreating Panzer Army Afrika.

Hitler's obsession with his southern flank continued, however, and he swiftly ordered large reinforcements. The distance from Sicily to north-east Tunisia was not far and, suddenly, Axis supply lines had shortened. Men, machines and aircraft were all hurried to form a bridgehead. It was also winter, and in the Mediterranean north of the country it soon began to rain and temperatures dropped. What had seemed like an easy victory slipped from the Allies' grasp.

By the third week of January 1943, Eighth Army had reached Tripoli then paused to regather strength. It was their turn to be a long way from their supply base – nearly 1,000 miles, in fact. Rommel, now greatly reinforced and with a second Axis army in northern Tunisia, chose this moment to strike back. On 14 February, he attacked the Americans advancing eastwards into southern Tunisia, pushing them back in disarray through the Kasserine Pass.

It was a great shock for the still inexperienced Americans, but the Axis counter-attack soon ran out of steam as Allied reinforcements were flung in to stop the rot. By 22 February Rommel's last-ditch attempt to affect the outcome in Africa had come to a halt.

American tanks: Stuart, top, and Grant, bottom.

Still Hitler sent more reinforcements to Tunisia. General Alexander had become 18th Army Group Commander, while the American General Dwight D. Eisenhower was promoted to Supreme Allied Commander. Alexander swiftly reorganized the front, sending green American units such as the 34th 'Red Bull' Division, who had suffered badly at Fondouk, off for battle-conditioning training. General George S. Patton took over command of II Corps after his predecessor, the hopeless General Lloyd Fredendall, was sacked.

Rommel made one last attempt to stem the advance of Eighth Army, but his counter-attack at Medenine on the south-east Tunisian border was swiftly defeated and on 6 March 1943 he left Africa for the last time, replaced by the Italian General Giovanni Messe.

Montgomery's next obstacle was the fixed defences between the coast and the Matmata Hills. While half his force headed towards the Mareth Line, the newly formed New Zealand Corps advanced wide into the desert in a 200-mile march around the back of the Matmata Hills and attacked through the Tebaga Gap. Despite a cumbersome armoured assault on the Mareth Line, this two-fisted punch, once again supported by the indefatigable Desert Air Force, was too much for the renamed Italian Panzer Army. By 27 March, Messe's troops were in retreat with Eighth Army following fast.

The Allies had now created the North African Tactical Air Force under 'Mary' Coningham, while both Eighth Army and a rejuvenated First Army were ready to close the net. Facing them was General Jürgen von Arnim's Fifth Panzer Army in the north and Messe's army now behind a new defensive line at Wadi Akarit north of Gabès. The endgame in North Africa was about to be played out.

Battle of the Tebaga Gap.

Despite the brilliant work of the 4th Indian Division, who attacked through the mountains and outflanked the Wadi Akarit position, Eighth Army's X Corps was too slow to take advantage and so a golden opportunity to encircle and destroy the Italian Panzer Army was missed. With US II Corps attacking from the west, they finally linked up with Eighth Army, who now pursued Messe's forces northwards towards Enfidaville, where they were finally checked.

Throughout April 1943, the fighting continued as the two Axis forces were pushed back into an ever-narrowing bridgehead in the north-east of the country. Hitler continued to pour supplies into Tunisia, mostly now by air. It was a disastrous policy. On 16 April, the US 57th Fighter Group shot down seventy-four enemy aircraft, most of which were transports. 'What a day!' noted pilot Dale Deniston in his diary. 'What a day for making history!' It became known as the 'Palm Sunday Turkey Shoot'.

Meanwhile, the 34th Red Bulls had returned from Battle School and managed to knock the Germans off the key Hill 609. The Americans were learning fast. US II Corps was now transferred to the north, Eighth Army held the line at Enfidaville, while several units, including the 4th Indian Division, were transferred to First Army for Operation VULCAN, the final assault in Tunisia.

The key attack was through the Medjerda Valley, which led directly to Tunis. The battle plan was the brainchild of the 4th Indians' commander, Major-General Francis Tuker, and was the perfect blend of massive firepower and infantry moving stealthily forward and surprising the enemy.

USAAF P-38 Lightnings and RAF Spitfires wreak havoc during the Palm Sunday Turkey Shoot off Cap Bon.

Today, the Battle of Medjerda is almost entirely forgotten, but it was fought against highly disciplined German troops and was one of the most perfectly executed battles the British carried out in the entire war. In the early hours of 6 May, massed night-bombers pummelled the German positions, followed by devastating artillery firing in concentrations on to one target after another – as should have been done at Alamein. Then 4th Indian Division attacked with stealth through long, reedy grass, achieving complete surprise. Many of the German units simply cut and ran, but as they fled they were hounded by yet more aircraft. A massive hole had been blown in the Axis defences and the road to Tunis was now open.

The city fell the next day, 7 May, while the Americans captured the second city, Bizerte. Axis resistance was crumbling fast. The Axis commander, General von Arnim, surrendered, rather fittingly, to General Tuker in the Cap Bon peninsula on 12 May, while General Messe signed the surrender document the following day. Some 250,000 Axis troops were taken prisoner, more than at Stalingrad in February of that year, along with a mass of aircraft, tanks, guns and ships. It was a major Allied victory.

At 1.16 p.m. on 13 May, General Alexander signalled to Winston Churchill: 'Sir, it is my duty to report that the Tunisian campaign is over. All enemy resistance has ceased. We are masters of the North African shores.'

General von Arnim surrendering to General Tuker.

Further Reading

GENERAL HISTORIES

James Holland *Together We Stand: North Africa 1942–1943 – Turning the Tide in the West* (HarperCollins, 2006)

James Holland *The War in the West: The Rise of Germany, 1939–1941* (Corgi, 2016)

James Holland *The War in the West: The Allies Strike Back, 1941–1943* (Corgi, 2017)

James Holland *Fortress Malta: An Island Under Siege, 1940–1943* (Weidenfeld & Nicolson, 2009)

W. G. F. Jackson *The North African Campaign, 1940–1943* (Batsford, 1975)

Robert M. Citino *Death of the Wehrmacht: The German Campaigns of 1942* (University Press of Kansas, 2007)

Robert M. Citino *The Wehrmacht Retreats: Fighting a Lost War, 1943* (University Press of Kansas, 2012)

MEMOIRS

Keith Douglas *Alamein to Zem Zem* (Faber, 2011)

Hans von Luck *Panzer Commander* (Cassell, 2002)

James Holland (ed.) *An Englishman at War: The Wartime Diaries of Stanley Christopherson* (Bantam, 2015)

Basil Liddell Hart (ed.) *The Rommel Papers* (Da Capo, 1982)

Lord Tedder *With Prejudice* (Cassell, 1966)

Count Galeazzo Ciano *Diaries, 1939–1943* (Doubleday, 1946)

FICTION

James Holland *The Burning Blue* (Arrow, 2004)

James Holland *Hellfire* (Corgi, 2012)

Penelope Lively *Moon Tiger* (Penguin, 2006)